24.00

Animal Sharpshooters

This brightly colored chameleon is just one of the amazing animals found on Earth.

Contents

Animal Sharpshooters

Anthony D. Fredericks

Watts LIBRARY

Franklin Watts
A Division of Grolier Publishing
New York • London • Hong Kong • Sydney
Danbury, Connecticut

For Marilyn Daly—extraordinary biologist, accomplished artist, dedicated colleague, and warm friend

The author would like to extend his sincere appreciation to Dr. Kathy Carlstead at the National Zoo in Washington, D.C., who reviewed the text for scientific accuracy. Her pertinent comments and professional advice were invaluable during the revision process.

Note to readers: Definitions for words in **bold** can be found in the Glossary at the back of this book.

The photo on the cover shows a chameleon catching an insect. The photo on page 2 shows a cone shell hunting a fish.

Photographs ©: Animals Animals: 36 (Anthony Bannister), 27 (M. Fogden), 34 (Keith Gillett), 14 (Raymond A. Mendez), 26 (Bertram G. Murray, Jr.), 46 (Fred Whitehead); BBC Natural History Unit: 19 (John Cancalosi), 31 (Jurgen Freund), 6 (Nick Garbutt), 12, 13 (Pete Oxford); ENP Images: 10 (Gerry Ellis); Norbert Wu Photography: 5 bottom, 33, 42, 44, 46 inset; Photo Researchers: cover (A. Cosmos Blank), 9 (Scott Camazine), 2 (Chester), 5 top, 22 (Ray Coleman), 41 (Stephen Dalton), 32, 39 (E. R. Degginger), 18 (Craig K. Lorenz), 50 (Tom McHugh), 20 (Richard Parker), 24 (National Audubon Society/S. J. Krasemann); Tom Stack & Associates: 21 (Chip & Jill Isenhart), 38 (Joe McDonald), 48 (Bob McKeever); Visuals Unlimited: 28 (Daniel W. Gotshall), 35 (A. Kerstitch), 30 (Ken Lucas), 17 (Rick Poley).

Visit Franklin Watts on the Internet at:
http://publishing.grolier.com

Library of Congress Cataloging-in-Publication Data

Fredericks, Anthony D.
    Animal sharpshooters / Anthony D. Fredericks.
        p.   cm.— (Watts Library)
    Includes bibliographical references and index.
    Summary: Describes animals, such as horned lizards, bolas spiders, cobras, and archerfish, that survive by throwing something to either catch prey or to avoid being captured by their enemies.
    ISBN 0-531-11700-6 (lib. bdg.)   0-531-16417-9 (pbk.)
    1. Animal defenses—Juvenile literature [1. Animal defenses.] I. Title. II. Series.
QL759.F72   1999
591.47—dc21   98-30028
                                                                    CIP
                                                                            AC

Why Sharpshooters Shoot

Think about the incredible variety of animals in the world. The millions and millions of **species** of animals on land, in the air, and in the sea come in an amazing assortment of shapes, sizes, and colors.

Some of these animals are familiar. They live with you, or you've seen them on television or in a zoo. But most are less familiar. They live in other countries, or they don't often appear in the books and magazines you read.

Whether or not an animal species is familiar to you, one thing is certain: it has developed special traits or behaviors that helped it survive for thousands—maybe even millions—of years. A trait or behavior that helps an animal survive is called an **adaptation**. It helps an animal adapt—or adjust—to its environment. An adaptation may allow a species to move more efficiently, feed on certain **prey**, or protect itself in an unusual or effective way.

Many animals spend most of the time they're awake looking for food or trying to avoid enemies. Some animals have learned to capture prey by throwing something at it. For example, the archerfish spits water at insects to knock them into the water where the fish can eat them. A web-throwing spider casts a net over its victims—trapping them until they can be killed and eaten.

Other animals throw things at their enemies to protect themselves. For example, one kind of Australian termite uses a nozzle on its head to squirt a gooey substance that traps would-be attackers. The bombardier beetle squirts a cloud of poisonous gas at its enemies and then hurries away while its enemy is blinded. When the sea cucumber feels threatened, it tosses its entire stomach at an approaching **predator**. While the enemy is distracted, the sea cucumber makes a run for it.

All these animals have developed unusual ways of protecting themselves from enemies. These adaptations, which help

Nasutitermes soldier termites use their nozzle-shaped heads to spray a sticky liquid at their enemies.

animals survive in the wild, have developed over hundreds or thousands of years through a process called **evolution.** Evolution is the gradual change of living things into new forms. Species that do not evolve or change over time may die out. An animal that develops a useful adaptation is more likely to survive and reproduce.

The evolutionary process has also helped some animals develop into many different species. For example, many scien-

A chameleon can change the color of its skin to match its surroundings.

tists believe that modern-day birds are descendants of the dinosaurs that lived millions of years ago. This natural process has produced some truly amazing animals.

One incredible animal is the chameleon, a kind of lizard that is best known for its amazing skin. The chameleon can change its skin color to match its surroundings. For example, if a chameleon is resting on a green plant, its skin becomes green. If it is resting on a brown tree, its skin color changes to brown. A chameleon can also change its skin color in response to sunlight or temperature. It can even change color when something frightens it.

Chameleons prey mainly on insects, spiders, and other small invertebrates (animals without backbones). Some larger species of

A chameleon's tongue is long, strong, and incredibly quick in catching a fly.

chameleons hunt small birds, mammals, and other lizards. The chameleon is very patient. When it spots a likely meal, it stares at the prey for a long time before attacking. Its attack, however, is quick. The chameleon's tongue shoots out at an incredible speed.

Usually, the victim is trapped on the sticky tip of the chameleon's tongue and pulled back into the chameleon's mouth. The action is so fast that the prey has no chance to escape. Powerful muscles and a specially shaped bone in the

chameleon's mouth contribute to the speed of this action. A chameleon's tongue can be fully extended to the length of its body in one-sixteenth of a second and can be pulled back in one-fourth of a second. That's faster than you can blink your eyes.

A chameleon's tongue is one of the fastest-moving body parts in the animal kingdom. The chameleon is probably one of nature's best-known "sharpshooters." But other creatures, in other ways, are just as amazing.

The Texas horned lizard distracts its enemies by shooting a stream of blood from its eyes.

Chapter One

Gross Shooters

If you were attacked by an enemy, how would you protect yourself? Would you throw something at the enemy? Would you fight or would you run away?

Scientists have learned that many species of animals have developed some special—and sometimes very unusual—ways of protecting themselves. These animals discharge substances from their bodies to confuse or temporarily blind their attackers. To us, the thought of throwing **feces** (solid body wastes), squirting blood, or firing hot gases is gross, but that is how some creatures protect themselves in a dangerous world.

Rear Ended

One of nature's most unusual animals is the skipper butterfly. Skippers are in a class by themselves. They look like moths, but have traits of both butterflies and moths. The adults are stocky with large heads, thick bodies, and short wings. The butterfly's name comes from its rapid, bouncy flight. The skipper butterfly seems to skip over meadows and fields.

Scientists have been studying ways to control skippers because they are agricultural pests. When researchers began looking closely at the life cycle of this creature, they discovered something quite amazing.

Like other butterflies and moths, skippers begin their lives as caterpillars. Because slow-moving caterpillars are a favorite prey for birds and other meat-eating insects, the skipper has an ability that helps it fool its enemies. To find caterpillars, many predators home in on the smell of their feces. The skipper caterpillar can shoot its **fecal bullets** (pellets of its solid body wastes) up 6.5 feet (2 meters), so when a predator zeroes in on the pellets, it won't find a caterpillar.

To prepare for "firing," the skipper caterpillar releases a fecal pellet. This pellet rests in a little cup near the opening at the end of the **alimentary canal,** or **rectum.** The caterpillar begins to build up blood pressure around the rectum. When the pressure is sufficient, the pellet explodes from the rectum and shoots through the air. If necessary, the caterpillar can quickly "reload" and fire a string of pellets in a fairly short amount of time. This unusual adaptation has helped ensure the survival of the skipper.

The Eyes Have It

The horned lizard might remind you of the dragons you have seen in storybooks. Its fearsome appearance, squat form, and head armor make it look more scary than it really is.

Although horned lizards are often called horned toads, they are much more closely related to chameleons than common toads. There are fourteen species of horned lizards on Earth.

Does a horned lizard remind you of a dragon?

All of them live in the western parts of the United States and Mexico. They prefer desert and semidesert areas.

Horned lizards have few enemies. Sometimes a desert snake or another desert creature will approach a horned lizard, thinking it is a slow-moving and easy-to-catch meal. But the horned lizard has a most unusual defense—it squirts blood from the corners of its eyes.

An approaching predator or intruder might hesitate, frightened by the squirting blood. That delay gives the horned lizard just enough time to burrow under the sand or scurry to safety under a nearby rock. The squirted blood does not have to hit the would-be predator to be effective. The squirted blood may simply draw the predator's attention away from the horned lizard. It is this unexpected action that gives the horned lizard time to escape.

After a horned lizard discharges blood from its eye, it runs away from its enemy.

Rapid Fire

Have you ever seen a war movie in which a soldier was firing a machine gun at the enemy—RAT-A-TAT-TAT, RAT-A-TAT-TAT? The firing action is so rapid that it seems to be nonstop. Believe it or not, the bombardier beetle does almost the same thing when an enemy approaches.

The bombardier beetle is a common name for a group of ground beetles that are about 0.5 to 1 inch (1 to 2.5 cm) long. Whenever a bombardier beetle feels threatened, it turns around so that its rear end is pointed in the direction of its enemy. Then it ejects a hot spray from its **anus**—the opening

The bombardier beetle can be described as a walking machine gun.

Beetle Mania

Scientists estimate that there are more than 400,000 different species of beetles in the world. In fact, new species of beetles are being discovered every year.

The largest beetle is the male Hercules beetle of Central America (right), which can reach a length of 2.5 inches (6 cm). The smallest beetle is the feather-winged beetle, which is smaller than the period at the end of this sentence.

Some beetles are plant eaters, others are meat eaters, and a few eat the remains of dead animals.

at the end of the alimentary canal. When the beetle's spray hits the air, it makes a popping sound and turns into a gas. The predator is blinded by the gas and confused by the noise.

The bombardier beetle can fire up to 500 times a second. People who mishandle this sharpshooter have been temporarily blinded by the gas.

Ogre-eyed spiders have large eyes that help them see in dim light.

Chapter Two

Free Throw Experts

How do you get food to eat? If you're like most people, you, or someone in your family, shops for food at the supermarket and then prepares it. Obtaining the food you need doesn't really take much of your time.

Many animals spend most of their waking hours hunting for food. To be successful hunters, they must have traits that help them. If an animal's prey comes out at night, the animal must be able to find its prey in the dark. It should have good hearing or super-sensitive eyes. If an animal's prey lives in trees, the animal must be able to move quickly without falling. Adaptations like these ensure the continuing survival of a species.

Cowboy Spider

All orb weavers spin complex webs made up of concentric circles. This spider has caught a moth in its web.

The bolas spider is found throughout Africa, Australia, and the United States. It is part of a large group of spiders known as orb weavers—spiders that use silk to build webs in **concentric** circles. The webs are held together with several radiating lines.

The bolas spider is one animal that has turned hunting into an art. In fact, it has developed a specialized weapon to capture its prey. Unlike other orb weavers, the bolas spider does something quite unusual—it lassos its victims! It is one of the few animal species that has evolved to use a "tool" to catch its food.

At dusk, a bolas spider crawls to the edge of its web and hangs from one of the horizontal threads. It begins to twirl a line of silk like a cowboy twirls a lasso. This line of silk has a small sticky drop at the end. As a male moth flies by, it is attracted by a special chemical in the drop. It flies too close and gets snared on the sticky blob. Then spider the reels in the fluttering moth and devours it.

Recently, scientists have discovered some unusual things about the bolas spider: only female bolas spiders do the lassoing, and only male moths are attracted to the chemicals in the sticky drop.

The bolas spider is not always successful in capturing its prey. If it doesn't catch a moth within an hour or so, the spider rolls its line into a ball and eats it. The spider then spins a

This bolas spider is wrapping up a freshly caught moth.

new line with another sticky blob at the end and waits again for a passing moth. It is a **nocturnal** hunter; during the day the bolas spider clings to the edge of a branch and remains motionless. It looks a lot like a flower bud or a bird dropping, so predators usually don't notice it.

Just Dropping In

The web-throwing spider lives in tropical and subtropical regions of the world. This spider is often referred to as the ogre-eyed spider because it has ugly facial features and two enormous eyes. The eyes are capable of seeing in very dim light. This is a handy adaptation because the web-throwing spider does all its hunting at night.

The web-throwing spider lives on the branches of rain forest trees. During the day, when it is resting, the spider extends its legs and lies flat against a branch. To any passing predator, it looks exactly like a small twig or part of a tree branch.

After dusk, the web-throwing spider spins a tiny, tightly woven web between its front legs. Hanging head down on a silken thread, the spider holds its miniature net and waits for a passing insect. When an insect walks underneath, the web-throwing spider opens its tiny net, drops it over the prey, and quickly scoops it up. All this happens in the blink of an eye—well before the unfortunate victim has a chance to escape.

The web-throwing spider is a sharpshooter because it captures its prey with quick and deadly accuracy. Its lightning-fast reactions, combined with a specialized "tool," are the keys to its survival. This spider has adapted to its environment by evolving a special way of obtaining its food.

Lots of Light

The eyes of a web-throwing spider absorb 2,000 times more light than the eyes of any other spider.

A web-throwing spider prepares a trap.

27

Some sea cucumbers shoot their guts at predators.

Chapter Three

Underwater Shooters

The ocean is filled with an incredible mix of fascinating, delightful, and horrifying living things. It is home to some of the most unusual creatures in the world. Some of these are harmless, others are dangerous, and a few are just plain weird.

These creatures include the sea cucumber, which literally spills its guts for protection. There are more than 1,100 species of sea cucumber throughout the world! The ocean is also home to the beautiful but deadly cone shell snail, which uses a poisoned barb to kill its prey. Cone shell snails can be found in tropical and subtropical oceans around the world. These creatures are among the most amazing sharp-shooters on Earth.

No Guts!

The sea cucumber may look like something that grows in your garden, but it is actually an animal. Sea cucumbers are members of a group of animals known as **echinoderms**, or spiny-skinned animals. Other members of this group include sand dollars, sea urchins, and sea stars. All echinoderms live on the ocean floor.

Sea cucumbers have leathery, warty bodies shaped like cucumbers and rows of tiny tube feet with suction disks on

A warty sea cucumber moves slowly across the ocean floor.

their flat underside. They use their tube feet to drag themselves over the seafloor.

At one end of the sea cucumber is the mouth, which is surrounded by several **tentacles.** Most sea cucumbers eat mud, small plants and animals, or sand. Some burrowing sea cucumbers swallow sand as they plow through it, digesting any edible matter it contains.

At the other end of the sea cucumber is the anus, which serves two purposes. It discharges body wastes, and it is used for breathing. Most sea cucumbers breathe by pulling water into the anus and the body cavity. There, the seawater mixes with body fluids and supplies the creature with the oxygen it needs.

The main enemies of sea cucumbers are sea stars and certain types of bottom-dwelling fish. Because the sea cucumber is slow-moving, it has developed two very unusual methods for defending itself from these predators. These defenses classify the sea cucumber as a sharpshooter.

If a sea cucumber is threatened by an approaching predator, it discharges all

Yum, Yum

Sea cucumbers may not look appetizing to us, but in the Far East and the South Pacific they are considered a great delicacy. There, they are grown, harvested, and served at the dinner table. They may be eaten raw or dried and used to make soups.

The bronze-spotted cucumber lives in the Great Barrier Reef, a huge coral reef off the coast of Australia. It launches long sticky threads at its enemies.

Hiding Out

Some species of sea cucumber provide shelter and protection for a tiny fish known as a pearlfish. This fish is small enough to slip into the sea cucumber's anal opening. It hides there with just the tip of its head sticking out.

its internal organs. In other words, it spills its guts! The organs are shot out from its anus. Depending on the size of the predator, the organs either completely cover it or stick to its sides. Often, the predator is so surprised by this that it hesitates or stops its attack. The predator may even decide to swim off in the opposite direction. Meanwhile, the sea cucumber burrows into the sand or hides beneath a rock. There, it spends the next few days regrowing a whole new set of internal organs.

Some species of sea cucumbers use a different trick to escape from enemies. Instead of spilling their guts, they squirt long sticky threads from their anus. The attacker becomes entangled in these threads. While it tries to get loose, the sea cucumber gets away. Unfortunately, the sea cucumber cannot retract these threads, so it must grow an entire new set.

Straight Shooter

Lots of people enjoy collecting seashells. Fascinating colors, a variety of shapes and sizes, and intricate patterns make shell collecting an exciting hobby. But there's one shell you don't want to collect with the animal inside. It's one of the most beautiful—and most prized—shells in the world, but it also houses one of the most dangerous animals on Earth. It's the cone shell snail—a kind of sea snail named for the shape of its shell.

Cone shell snails can be found in tropical and subtropical oceans around the world—from Hawaii to Australia to the Indian Ocean. They live in shallow waters or coral reefs. Depending on the species, they range in size from less than 1 inch to 9 inches (2.5 to 23 cm) long.

When a cone snail's prey gets close enough, the ferocious predator slowly slides a special fleshy tube called a

The cone shell may be beautiful, but it is also dangerous.

This cone shell has extended its fleshy proboscis. Is it about to attack a victim?

proboscis toward its victim and attacks. Before the victim can sense the danger it is in, the snail contracts its muscles so a milky white poison fills a hollow barb inside the snail's proboscis. A moment later, the snail shoots its prey with the poisoned barb.

The prey dies almost instantly. (If a human being is the victim, death occurs in just a few minutes.) Then the poison begins digesting the victim from the inside out. After a while,

This cone shell has caught a small fish and is trying to engulf it.

the snail enlarges its mouth and begins to engulf the victim. Swallowing and digestion may take several hours.

Collecting shells can be a fun and exciting hobby, but be careful not to add this sharpshooter to your collection!

The mocambique
spitting cobra can be
found in South Africa.

Chapter Four

Speedy Spitters

Is it polite to spit? Of course not! Anyway, spitting isn't something that most human beings do on a regular basis. But spitting is a survival strategy for some animals. Some animals spit to obtain food, while others spit to protect themselves from enemies.

Spitting Power

One of the most feared of all snakes, the cobra, is often portrayed in books and

This Egyptian banded cobra is expanding its neck skin into a hood.

movies as an extremely deadly creature—and with good reason. Cobras, which are found throughout the Philippines, Africa, and southern Asia, are well-known for their intimidating behavior and fatal bite. Their flaring hoods and their menacing glare make them easy to recognize.

Cobras are classified as venomous, or poisonous, snakes. A **venom** is a poison produced by an animal to paralyze or kill another animal. Cobra venom is known as a **neurotoxin** because it acts on the nervous system. It causes paralysis, nausea, breathing difficulties, and eventually death through heart and breathing failure.

A cobra's venom is secreted from glands that lie just below its eyes. The venom runs down **ducts** (small tubes) to two fangs that grow from the front of the upper jaw. These fangs are like the needles your doctor uses to give you a shot. A cobra's fangs are designed to puncture a victim's flesh and inject a deadly poison as rapidly as possible.

In Africa, two types of cobras—the ringhals and black-necked cobras—are also known as spitting cobras. They spit at enemies when they feel threatened.

Most cobras have a canal inside each fang through which their venom passes. In spitting cobras, the canal goes through the fang but does not stop there. At the tip of each fang, the canal turns sharply and ends at the front of the fang. When surprised, this cobra rears up, opens its mouth, and forces

Long Distance

The king cobra is the world's longest venomous snake. Most are about 13 feet (4 m) in length, but some are up to 18 feet (5.5 m) long.

A ringhal cobra prepares to strike.

Right on Target

Spitting cobras are powerful spitters. They can hit targets up to 13 feet (4 m) away.

venom out of its fangs and onto its victim. It uses strong muscles surrounding the poison gland to push out the poison.

A spitting cobra aims its spray at the eyes of its victim. The venom causes intense pain and may even blind the attacker. If a human being is the victim, the venom must be washed out quickly. This is definitely one sharpshooter you don't want to meet eye to eye.

Spit at Your Dinner!

An amazing fish lives in the shallow waters of Southeast Asia. In one respect, the archerfish is unlike any other fish you've ever met—it spits at its dinner to catch it! And it almost always succeeds!

The archerfish's diet consists mainly of small water animals and insects that swim or float in brackish water. But archerfish also shoot down insects. To do this, the fish positions itself just below the surface, with the tip of its mouth barely breaking through the water. Using its large eyes, its ability to focus well, and its skill at judging distances accurately, the archerfish watches for an unsuspecting insect on a leaf or twig hanging over the water.

Where Archerfish Live

Six different species of archerfish live in Southeast Asia. They can be found in saltwater mangrove swamps and shallow seas as well as in freshwater streams. They live in India, the Malay Archipelago, and in parts of Australia and the Philippines.

Then the archerfish attacks its prey. First, it compresses its gill covers very rapidly. This forces water into the fish's mouth. At the same time, the fish presses its tongue upward—converting a groove in the roof of its mouth into a thin tube. This creates a powerful stream of water that is forcefully pushed out of the fish's mouth.

This stream of water hits the unsuspecting insect and knocks it into the water. The archerfish hurries to where the insect has landed and quickly gobbles it up. If the archerfish misses the insect with the first jet of water droplets, it shoots out several more in rapid succession. Once a victim has been targeted, it doesn't have a chance. An archerfish can hit a small insect up to 6.6 feet (2 m) away.

This sharpshooter— the archerfish—rarely misses a target.

Archerfish learn to "spit" when they are very young, and their marksmanship tends to improve with age—and practice. This amazing ability suggests that archerfish may be relatively intelligent creatures. Of course, the opposite could be said about a human being who spits!

When a dog wags its tail it is a sign of friendliness, not danger.

Chapter Five

Tail Gunners

Have you ever watched a dog wag its tail? Most dogs wag their tails when they're happy or excited. A dog might wag its tail when its owner comes home at the end of the day or when it is given a special treat. This wagging tail is a sure sign of happiness, so it is always a welcome sight.

Not all animals act like dogs. Some move their tails not because they are happy, but because they are threatened or angry. Their tails are used as weapons to defend them from their enemies or as tools to capture approaching prey. One thing is for sure—you don't want to be around when these animals wag *their* tails!

Stingrays are found in many oceans around the world.

Terrible Tails

If you were shooting an arrow at a target, how often do you think you would hit the bull's-eye—the center of the target? You're about to meet an animal that can hit the target every single time. Unfortunately, that target is often someone's foot or leg.

The stingray is a marine creature that spends its entire life on the ocean floor resting or looking for food. There are approximately 400 different species of stingrays throughout the world. They can be found in shallow tropical or temperate oceans. These scary-looking ocean predators rarely go deeper than 427 feet (130 m) below the water's surface.

Stingrays are closely related to sharks and skates. They have a flattened, circular shape with winglike **pectoral** fins along their sides. They travel by using their pectoral fins to make wavelike movements. If you can imagine a dinner plate skimming across the ocean floor, you will have a pretty good idea of what a stingray looks like.

The stingray's most distinctive—and most dangerous—feature is its tail. This tail, which is almost as long as the stingray's body, has a single poisonous spike that may up to 14.6 inches

Lightweights and Heavyweights

The smallest species of stingray is about 12 inches (30 cm) across and weighs about 1.1 pounds (0.5 kilograms). The largest stingrays measure about 16.4 feet (5 m) across and weighs nearly 750 pounds (340 kg).

45

The stingray attacks enemies with its long tail. A spike on the tail (inset) contains poison that can cause sharp pain, throbbing, and breathing difficulties in people.

(37 cm) long. The spike is lined with saw-toothed edges and a series of poison-filled grooves. The stingray uses its tail to protect itself when it is attacked or disturbed.

People sometimes encounter stingrays as they walk in shallow water near an ocean beach. If a person steps on a stingray, the creature lashes out at lightning speed with its powerful tail. The stingray's spine may strike the person's foot or lower leg. Unlike a bee's stinger, however, the stingray's spine isn't left behind.

The spine cuts and tears the victim's flesh while injecting a powerful poison. The poison's effects are immediate and long-lasting. The victim typically experiences sharp pains, an intense throbbing around the wound, and breathing difficulties. In some cases, the poison affects the heartbeat or nervous system and may even be fatal.

Stingrays use their whiplike tails primarily for defense. Usually, they are quite content to glide across the ocean floor looking for small clams, crabs, fish or other animals to eat. But if you see a stingray, stay away! This sharpshooter never misses its target!

A scorpion is a fierce-looking creature that can be deadly.

Creepy Crawler

Although the scorpion is one of the most feared desert creatures, only a few of the more than 9,000 species of scorpions are dangerous to humans. And, strangely enough, it's the small scorpions—ones about 1 inch (2.5 cm) long—that are most dangerous.

Scorpions are found in most of the warmer regions of the world. In the United States, they thrive in desert areas and have been seen as far north as Oregon. They are primarily nocturnal animals. During the day, they hide under logs or large rocks.

Scorpions have poor eyesight—even though some species have as many as twelve eyes. Because they hunt at night, they rely on their sense of touch to locate prey. Typically, a scorpion walks around with its claws spread apart until it bumps into a tasty spider or insect. Then, the scorpion's claws snap shut and the victim is torn to pieces or crushed. The scorpion doesn't eat the victim; instead, it sucks the victim's body juices.

If the prey is large or puts up a fight, the scorpion may use its powerful stinger. A scorpion's stinger is a hollow tube connected to a poison gland near the end of its tail. The scorpion's muscles force the stinger into the body of its prey. Then the scorpion squeezes poison from the gland down the hollow tube and into the victim's body. The poison is powerful enough to **immobilize**—that is, paralyze—or kill any struggling victim.

They Come in All Sizes

The smallest scorpion in the world is only 0.2 inches (5 mm) long. That's smaller than the width of your little finger. The largest scorpion is 7.9 inches (20 cm) long.

Scorpions are related to crabs and lobsters. Many scientists call scorpions "living fossils" because they look very much like their ancestors did 395 million years ago.

A scorpion feasts on a cricket.

Scorpions like to sleep in warm, dark places. The danger for humans comes when they crawl into bedding or shoes, or sneak under carpets. A scorpion will lash out with its tail when a barefooted person steps on it. A scorpion will also strike when someone puts on a shoe it has decided to rest in!

Some scorpion stings can be fatal—particularly for children. The venom acts on the brain as well as the body. Victims often act crazy and may become violent. Profuse sweating, vomiting, and breathing difficulties may follow a scorpion's sting. A frothy liquid spills out of the victim's mouth, and blindness usually occurs. Death comes a few minutes or a few hours later.

A scorpion's stinger is lightning fast and deadly accurate. Although it's not used as often as some people believe, that doesn't mean that it's not dangerous.

Clearly, scorpions and stingrays have evolved adaptations that classify them as sharpshooters. These adaptations help them get the food they need, protect themselves from other animals, and allow them to stay alive long enough to reproduce. They, and the other sharpshooters described in this book, help to make our world an incredible and interesting place.

Glossary

adaptation—a change in a living thing that allows it to survive in a particular environment.

alimentary canal—the tube that carries food through the body.

anus—the body opening through which solid wastes are eliminated.

concentric—a series of circles that have the same center.

duct—a tube that carries a liquid or a gas.

echinoderm—a group of animals with spiny skins.

evolution—the process by which living things change over time.

fecal bullet—a small pellet of body waste released through the anus.

feces—solid body waste.

gaucho—a South American cowboy.

herpetologist—a scientist who studies amphibians and reptiles.

immobilize—to paralyze; to make something unable to move.

neurotoxin—a chemical that acts on the central nervous system.

nocturnal—most active at night.

pampa—a wide-open plain in South America.

pectoral—of or on the chest.

predator—an animal that hunts and eats other animals.

prey—an animal that is hunted and eaten by another animal.

proboscis—a nose or noselike appendage.

rectum—the end section of the alimentary canal.

species—a group of living things that have some common qualities.

tentacle—an arm or feeler used by an invertebrate to sense its surroundings.

venom—a poison produced inside the body of an animal.

To Find Out More

Books

Butterfield, Moira. *1000 Facts about Wild Animals*. New York: Kingfisher Books, 1992.

Fredericks, Anthony D. *Weird Walkers*. Minnetonka, MN: NorthWord Press, 1996.

_____. *Exploring the Rainforest*. Golden, CO: Fulcrum Publishing, 1996.

Maynard, Thane. *Animal Olympians*. New York: Franklin Watts, 1994.

Parsons, Alexandria. *Amazing Poisonous Animals*. New York: Alfred A. Knopf, 1990.

Silver, Donald M. *One Small Square: Seashore*. New York: Scientific American Books for Young Readers, 1993.

Magazine Articles

"Olympic Feats, Fins & Feathers: Wild Athletes of the Animal World." *Nature Conservancy*, vol. 46, no. 4 (July/August 1996), pp. 10–15.

"Scatapult." *Discover*, vol. 19, no. 4 (April 1998), p. 18.

Videos

Predators of North America. (Catalog No. A51180). Washington, DC: National Geographic Society, 1981.

Spiders: Aggression and Mating. (Catalog No. A51209). Washington, DC: National Geographic Society, 1974.

The World of Insects. (Catalog No. A51248). Washington, DC: National Geographic Society, 1979.

CD-ROMs

Amazon Trail (MECC, 6160 Summit Dr., N. Minneapolis, MN 55430). IBM & Macintosh [Grades 4–12].

Food Chains and Webs (Cyber Ed Inc., P.O. Box 3037, Paradise, CA 95967). IBM & Macintosh [Grades 6–12].

The San Diego Zoo Presents the Animals (Mindscape, 60 Leveroni Ct., Novato, CA 94949). IBM & Macintosh [Grades 1–8].

Organizations and Online Sites

Defenders of Wildlife
1101 14th Street, NW #1400
Washington, DC 20005
http://www.defenders.org/index.html

National Audubon Society
700 Broadway
New York, NY 10003-9562
http://www.audubon.com

National Wildlife Federation
8925 Leesburg Pike
Vienna, VA 22184-0001
http://www.nwf.org/

The Wildlife Conservation Society
2300 Southern Boulevard
Bronx, NY 10460
http://www.wcs.org

Young Entomologists' Society
6907 West Grand River Ave.
Lansing MI 48906-9131
http://insects.ummz.lsa.umich.edu/yes/yes.html

A Note
on Sources

I often get ideas for books by reading articles in a variety of science magazines. Some of my favorites include *Audubon*, *National Wildlife*, *International Wildlife*, *Nature Conservancy*, *Wildlife Conservation*, and *Discover*. To find more detailed information about specific animals or species, I often search on the Internet. I rely on the websites created and maintained by colleges, universities, or well-known organizations. I usually don't use information from personal websites because it may not be reliable.

Next, I talk to librarians. They help me find all kinds of resource materials to read. When I was working on this book, I read *The Way Nature Works* edited by Clifford Bishop, *Beastly Behaviors* by Janine Benyus, *Nature Got There First* by Phil Gates, *Biology of Animals* by Cleveland Hickman, *The Flight of the Iguana* and *Natural Acts* by David Quammen, and *Spineless Wonders* by Richard Conniff. I also read some nonfiction children's books by other authors such as Laurence Pringle, Seymour Simon, Gail Gibbons, Patricia Lauber, Sneed Collard, Donald Silver, and Ron Hirschi.

Since I teach full-time at York College in York, Pennsylvania, I often ask other professors questions. I also visit zoos, wildlife preserves, and aquariums to observe animals and ask more questions. Finally, I watch National Geographic television specials and some programs on the Discovery Channel. All this research is necessary to make sure that the information in my books (including this one) is accurate and up-to-date.

—*Anthony D. Fredericks*

Index

Numbers in *italics* indicate illustrations.

About the Author

Anthony D. Fredericks is nationally known for his energetic and highly practical presentations for strengthening elementary science instruction. His dynamic and stimulating seminars have captivated thousands of teachers from coast to coast.

His background includes extensive experience as a classroom teacher, author, professional storyteller, and university specialist in elementary science and language arts methods.

He has written more than forty books, including the best-selling *The Complete Science Fair Handbook*, which he co-authored with Isaac Asimov. His children's books on animals and the environment have been highly praised by teachers and librarians across the country. He is currently a Professor of Education at York College in York, Pennsylvania.